Straight to the Source

Internet

John Hamilton

ABDO
Publishing Company

visit us at
www.abdopub.com

Published by ABDO Publishing Company, 4940 Viking Drive, Edina, Minnesota 55435.
Copyright © 2005 by Abdo Consulting Group, Inc. International copyrights reserved in all countries. No part of this book may be reproduced in any form without written permission from the publisher. The Checkerboard Library™ is a trademark and logo of ABDO Publishing Company.

Printed in the United States.

Cover Photo: Corbis
Interior Photos: Corbis pp. 1, 5, 7, 9, 10, 11, 12, 13, 15, 18, 19, 21, 23, 25, 28, 29

Series Coordinator: Stephanie Hedlund
Editors: Kate A. Conley, Kristin Van Cleaf
Art Direction: Neil Klinepier

Library of Congress Cataloging-in-Publication Data

Hamilton, John, 1959-
    Internet / John Hamilton.
        p. cm. -- (Straight to the source)
    Summary: An overview of the internet, the world wide web, and email.
    ISBN 1-59197-544-1
    1. Internet--Juvenile literature. 2. Electronic mail messages--Juvenile literature. 3. World Wide Web--Juvenile literature. [1. Internet. 2. Email. 3. World Wide Web.] I. Title.

TK5105.875.I57H357 2004
004.67'8--dc22
                                                                2003057788

Contents

The Internet

The Internet is a powerful tool for sharing information. It is also a way for people to communicate with one another. E-mail, chat rooms, and instant messaging help people stay in touch.

People use the Internet for practical purposes, too. Some shop or bank **online** every day. Others order books, movie tickets, or almost anything you can imagine online.

The Internet is extensive. So, finding the information you need is like going on a treasure hunt. Luckily, there are tools to guide you in your search.

One of these tools is the World Wide Web. The Web helps people find information on the Net. It is proof that with the right tools and skills, you can locate almost anything on the Internet.

Opposite page: *The Internet is a great way to locate information such as maps for research projects.*

ARPANET

Today, the Internet is a **network** of thousands of computer networks all around the world. However, when it first began, the Internet was very small. It started as part of a United States Department of Defense project called ARPANET.

Dr. J.C.R. Licklider was the first person to guide the ARPANET team. Its job was to find ways to use **technology** to defend the United States. The military wanted to keep its computers running, even during a **nuclear** attack. To do this, ARPANET decided to build a computer network.

Members of the ARPANET team worked to make the network a reality. Dr. Leonard Kleinrock worked on ARPANET. He developed theories on packet switching technology.

EXTRA!

Packet Switching

Leonard Kleinrock developed the idea of packet switching. Packets are bits of information that are broken down from larger files. These bits are transferred from one computer to another and then put back together.

This technology was necessary because the original files were too large to travel the Internet. Networked computers had a much easier time transferring the smaller packets of information.

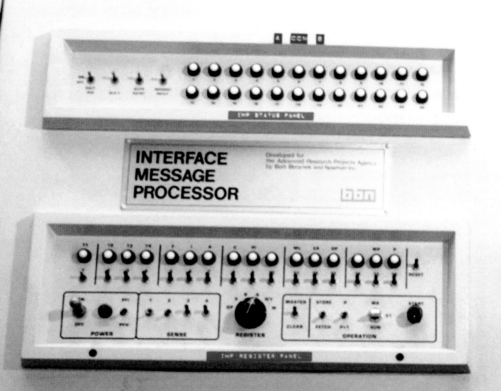

ARPANET used the Interface Message Processor (IMP) to route packets to the correct locations. Every computer site equipped with an IMP could send packets on the network.

Dr. Lawrence Roberts was another ARPANET team member. He helped turn Dr. Kleinrock's theories into a working computer **network**.

In 1969, three computers in California and one in Utah were networked together. ARPANET was successful. Soon, military computers were linked with those of companies and universities that worked with the Department of Defense.

During the 1970s, the network grew and improved. More and more computers were added. By 1981, ARPANET connected more than 200 computers.

ARPANET was supposed to have been just a military network. But, it soon linked many countries and universities. Scientists found it was an easy way to trade information.

Then in 1983, the U.S. military split off a section of ARPANET. MILNET became a separate network used just by the armed forces. ARPANET could then be used for scientific research, without concern about military secrecy.

ARPA
stands for "Advanced
Research Projects Agency."
Net stands for "network."
ARPANET was a
military network.

Today the letter D, which stands for
"Defense," has been added to ARPA.
DARPA's job is to find ways to use
new technology to defend the
United States.

NSFNet

In the mid-1980s, the National Science Foundation (NSF) built a more advanced computer **network**. It was called NSFNet. NSFNet linked university **supercomputer** centers that weren't already connected to ARPANET.

NSFNet's advanced network allowed anyone with a computer to use the Internet.

NSFNet helped scientists perform research. It acted as a backbone that linked other computer networks. As NSFNet grew, it quickly absorbed most of the networks that made up ARPANET. And in 1990, ARPANET was dissolved.

NSFNet had evolved to include companies as well as universities. The NSF soon stepped aside to let big companies, such as IBM and

MCI, run its **network**. This allowed the general population to have **access**, too.

In time, people started calling the network of networks the Internet. No one knows for sure who first used the term. It might have been Vinton Cerf, one of the founders of ARPANET. He is sometimes called the "Father of the Internet."

In the 1970s, Vinton Cerf helped develop TCP/IP. This stands for Transmission Control Protocol/Internet Protocol. It is a kind of language that different computer networks use to talk to one another. It is still the most widely used networking protocol today.

The Web

Many people think the Internet and the World Wide Web are the same thing. Actually, the Web is just one part of the Internet. There could be no Web without the Internet. But the Internet would exist without the Web.

The Web got its start in 1989 at CERN. CERN is a European group that does **nuclear** research. Its scientists wanted to find a way to quickly search for and share information. British computer scientist Tim Berners-Lee proposed a way of linking CERN data.

Berners-Lee found that with **hyperlinks**, scientists could find information from any computer on CERN's **network**. He knew the system could also work on the larger Internet.

This is one of the many computers at CERN. Today, CERN is known as the European Particle Physics Laboratory.

From left to right: *Vinton Cerf, Lawrence Roberts, Robert Kahn, and Tim Berners-Lee were recognized for their contributions to the Internet and World Wide Web in 2002.*

In 1990, Berners-Lee created the first browser with a GUI, or **graphical** user interface. He called it WorldWideWeb. Later, it was renamed Nexus so it would not be confused with the World Wide Web.

Nexus used **hypertext** markup language (HTML). This is the computer code in which Web pages are written. Web pages are text, sound, pictures, and even video that sit together in a file. These files appear on the Internet.

A collection of Web pages with a common subject is called a Web site. Web sites are connected by a system of **hypertext** and links. This system lets you quickly go from one page to another to find the information you're looking for.

Nexus and other browsers are programs that use the links to visit Web sites. These browsers are **graphical**. So, instead of just text, you can see and download photos, symbols, or even animation.

Computer programmers saw the potential of the World Wide Web. They developed several browsers, such as Viola and Cello. But, Mosaic was the easiest to use. So, it was popular with beginners.

By the late 1990s, the Web had exploded in popularity. It made the Internet easy to use, and more people wanted to get **online**.

Today, people continue to search the Internet. Mozilla, Internet Explorer, and Netscape are the most popular Web browsers. Apple's Safari browser is also becoming more widely used.

In the 1990s, many Web-based businesses, such as Amazon.com and eBay, were created.

Surfing the Net

In the 1990s, the Internet created an information revolution. A world of data was now available to almost anyone. It wasn't just for scientists anymore. Anyone with a computer could search the Internet.

By 1992, the Internet included more than 7,500 computer **networks**. These networks had thousands of **databases**. This made the Internet like an encyclopedia someone forgot to alphabetize.

Luckily, a new tool called a search engine was invented in the mid-1990s. A Web-based search engine makes it much easier to find Internet information. A search engine creates an index of Web sites with related information.

Soon after search engines were developed, metasearchers such as Dogpile were created. This **software** combines the results of several search engines into one list. Using a metasearcher is like fishing for information with a bigger net.

Opposite page: Google is a search engine used by many people today. Other search engines include AltaVista, Excite, and Lycos.

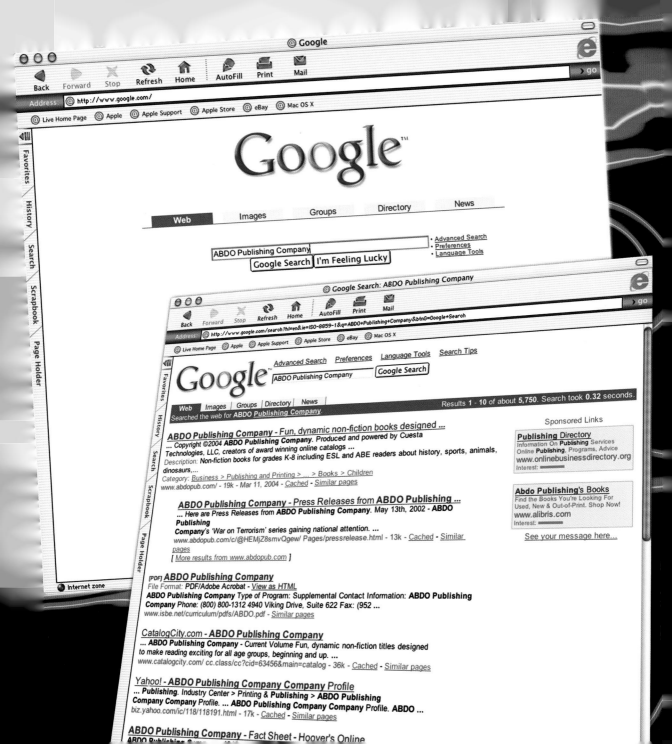

@ Google

Back   Forward   Stop   Refresh   Home   AutoFill   Print   Mail   › go

Address: @ http://www.google.com/

@ Live Home Page   @ Apple   @ Apple Support   @ Apple Store   @ eBay   @ Mac OS X

Favorites   History   Search   Scrapbook   Page Holder

Google™

Web   Images   Groups   Directory   News

· Advanced Search
· Preferences
· Language Tools

ABDO Publishing Company

Google Search   I'm Feeling Lucky

Internet zone

@ Google Search: ABDO Publishing Company

Back   Forward   Stop   Refresh   Home   AutoFill   Print   Mail   › go

Address: @ http://www.google.com/search?hl=en&ie=ISO-8859-1&q=ABDO+Publishing+Company&btnG=Google+Search

@ Live Home Page   @ Apple   @ Apple Support   @ Apple Store   @ eBay   @ Mac OS X

Favorites   History   Search   Scrapbook   Page Holder

Google™

Advanced Search   Preferences   Language Tools   Search Tips

ABDO Publishing Company   Google Search

Web   Images   Groups   Directory   News   Results **1 - 10** of about **5,750**. Search took **0.32** seconds.
Searched the web for ABDO Publishing Company.

ABDO Publishing Company - Fun, dynamic non-fiction books designed ...
... Copyright ©2004 **ABDO Publishing Company**. Produced and powered by Cuesta
Technologies, LLC, creators of award winning online catalogs ...
Description: Non-fiction books for grades K-8 including ESL and ABE readers about history, sports, animals,
dinosaurs,...
Category: Business > Publishing and Printing > ... > Books > Children
www.abdopub.com/ - 19k - Mar 11, 2004 - Cached - Similar pages

ABDO Publishing Company - Press Releases from **ABDO Publishing** ...
... Here are Press Releases from **ABDO Publishing Company**. May 13th, 2002 - **ABDO
Publishing
Company**'s 'War on Terrorism' series gaining national attention. ...
www.abdopub.com/c/@HEMjZ8smvQgew/ Pages/pressrelease.html - 13k - Cached - Similar
pages
[More results from www.abdopub.com]

[PDF] **ABDO Publishing Company**
File Format: PDF/Adobe Acrobat - View as HTML
ABDO Publishing Company Type of Program: Supplemental Contact Information: **ABDO Publishing
Company** Phone: (800) 800-1312 4940 Viking Drive, Suite 622 Fax: (952 ...
www.isbe.net/curriculum/pdfs/ABDO.pdf - Similar pages

CatalogCity.com - **ABDO Publishing Company**
... **ABDO Publishing Company** - Current Volume Fun, dynamic non-fiction titles designed
to make reading exciting for all age groups, beginning and up. ...
www.catalogcity.com/ cc.class/cc?cid=63456&main=catalog - 36k - Cached - Similar pages

Yahoo! - **ABDO Publishing Company Company** Profile
... **Publishing**. Industry Center > Printing & Publishing > **ABDO Publishing
Company Company** Profile. ... **ABDO Publishing Company Company** Profile. ABDO ...
biz.yahoo.com/ic/118/118191.html - 17k - Cached - Similar pages

ABDO Publishing Company - Fact Sheet - Hoover's Online

Then in 1994, David Filo and Jerry Yang created the Yahoo! **hierarchical** index. It is sometimes thought to

Yahoo!'s creators David Filo (left) *and Jerry Yang*

be a search engine. However, Yahoo! is different. It uses actual people, rather than **software**, to search for Web sites.

A Yahoo! index contains information found by librarians and experts. This makes the Web sites given more selective. Yahoo! is very popular. People search with it more than 200 million times each month.

Sometimes, searching the Internet is called "surfing the Net." To start surfing, have your Web browser go to your favorite search engine or index. Next, type in your subject's **keywords**.

In a few seconds, the search engine will find a list of Web sites that match your keywords. Search engines and hierarchical indexes act as magnets. If your topic is very general, such as "baseball," a search engine may point you to thousands of Web sites.

This information overload can be avoided. Narrow your search by adding more specific **keywords**. For example, type "baseball Minnesota Twins tickets," instead of just "baseball."

Your teacher or librarian may have great ideas for narrowing a search.

Narrowing Your Search

Searching the Internet is sometimes like being a magnet for Web sites. Advanced search options and Boolean operators are ways to narrow your search. Boolean operators are special words or symbols used by most search engines. They include AND, OR, and NOT. To be effective, they must be typed in capital letters.

◆ Typing "movie AND Disney" will only find Web sites that include both words. AND means that all the words in your search must be present.

◆ Typing "movie OR Disney" will find all Web sites that include either word or both of them. OR means that any of the words can be present.

◆ Typing "movie NOT Disney" will only find Web sites about movies that don't mention the word "Disney." NOT means that a word or phrase must not be included in search results.

Site Evaluation

While searching the Internet, you will find a lot of information. Unfortunately, it is easy to visit Web sites that are **biased** or incorrect. You must be very critical when deciding whether to use this information.

The first step in **evaluating** a Web site is to look at why it was made. It may have been developed to influence people. This could affect its **accuracy**. Government, university, and organization sites are usually more reliable than commercial sites.

The second step is to look at where the information comes from. This will help you determine whether the Web site is a reliable source. A personal Web site contains whatever its creator wants, so it may be inaccurate.

EXTRA!
Official Site Indicators

There are many Web sites available today. The best way to quickly identify who is responsible for the site is to look at its domain code. Domain codes are found in the URL. Here are some common domain codes and their meanings.

.edu = educational institution
.gov = government site
.org = organization or association site
.com = commercial site
.museum = museum site
.net = personal or other site

Finally, explore what others think of the site. Read a review in a **directory** to discover how experts view a site's information. Another way to check people's opinions is to visit the site's links. If the links go to credible sites, the source should be good, too.

When evaluating any source, ask yourself five questions. The questions are who, what, when, where, and why. Your answers will help you determine if a source is reliable.

E-mail

Today, one of the most popular uses of the Internet is e-mail. In fact, more e-mail is sent every year than is carried by all the world's postal systems combined. It is a communications **technology** that evolved along with the Internet.

University professors and students began sending messages to each other using ARPANET. Computer engineer Ray Tomlinson invented an easier e-mail system in 1971. He later added the @ symbol to e-mail addresses.

Today, e-mail can be a useful tool for research. It sends messages instantly to anyone in the world with an Internet connection. So, e-mail can be used to quickly contact experts and other professionals who live far away.

EXTRA!
Addresses and URLs

E-mail uses addresses much like the post office. Each part of an address stands for something. For example, in the e-mail address jdoe@abdopub.com, jdoe is the person's name. The symbol @ means at. And abdopub is the person's server, or location. This is followed by the domain code.

URLs are Web site addresses. The URL http://www.abdopub.com brings a visitor to that site. The http:// stands for the service. Next is the user, in this case the World Wide Web. Then abdopub is the server. Finally, there is the domain code.

E-mail often has attachments. Attachments can be text files, pictures, video files, or even computer programs.

E-mail can also be sent to many people at once by using a mailing list. E-mail sent to a mailing list reaches everyone who subscribes to it. This provides an opportunity to get feedback from many people without contacting them individually.

Newsgroups are also useful for mass mailing. They act like giant electronic bulletin boards. Experts in newsgroups answer many questions. So, these groups can be helpful when you are looking for information.

Netiquette

In 1968, J.C.R. Licklider and Robert Taylor published a paper. It was called "The Computer as a Communication Device." They wrote that the Internet is more than just an information **network**. It is a community made up of net citizens, or "netizens."

Licklider and Taylor wrote that each netizen contributes to the Internet's "virtual world." This way, the Internet becomes a more useful tool than anyone alone could create.

In order to be a good netizen, you should use netiquette. It is a set of manners and rules for behaving politely on the Internet. Using netiquette makes the Internet more pleasant and useful.

EXTRA!

Safety Netiquette

It is always a good idea to protect yourself when you are on the Internet. This "virtual world" can be dangerous. But, there are many ways to protect yourself.

★Don't use your full name in your e-mail address or screen name.

★Don't give anyone the password for your e-mail account.

★Never give your address or phone number to strangers.

★Never meet a stranger from the Internet alone.

The first rule of netiquette is to help newcomers, or newbies. Every Internet user was new once. And when newbies contribute to the Internet, it is an even more powerful tool.

Remember, you were a newbie once too! It is important to use netiquette with all Internet users.

It is good netiquette to research a question before asking an expert. Common questions are often posted on a page called Frequently Asked Questions (FAQ). FAQs save time and energy for everyone.

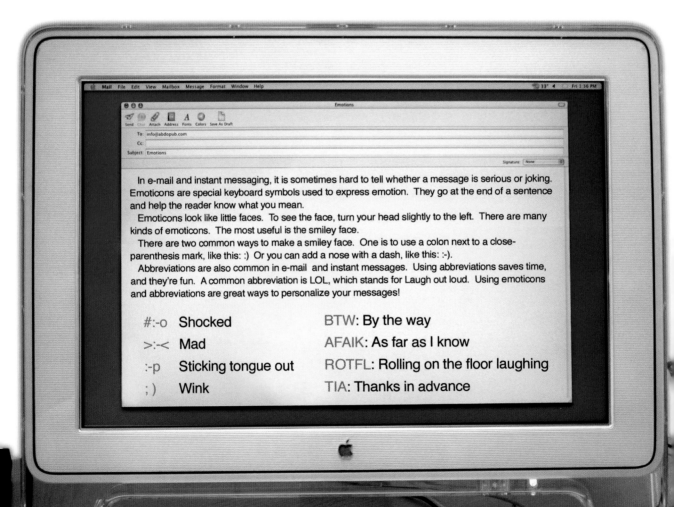

Mail File Edit View Mailbox Message Format Window Help

Emotions

Send Chat Attach Address Fonts Colors Save As Draft

To: info@abdopub.com
Cc:
Subject: Emotions

Signature: None

In e-mail and instant messaging, it is sometimes hard to tell whether a message is serious or joking. Emoticons are special keyboard symbols used to express emotion. They go at the end of a sentence and help the reader know what you mean.

Emoticons look like little faces. To see the face, turn your head slightly to the left. There are many kinds of emoticons. The most useful is the smiley face.

There are two common ways to make a smiley face. One is to use a colon next to a close-parenthesis mark, like this: :) Or you can add a nose with a dash, like this: :-).

Abbreviations are also common in e-mail and instant messages. Using abbreviations saves time, and they're fun. A common abbreviation is LOL, which stands for Laugh out loud. Using emoticons and abbreviations are great ways to personalize your messages!

#:-o   Shocked   BTW: By the way

>:-<   Mad   AFAIK: As far as I know

:-p   Sticking tongue out   ROTFL: Rolling on the floor laughing

;)   Wink   TIA: Thanks in advance

Good netiquette can be used when sending e-mail, too. It involves being brief and staying on topic. If you write about too many things, the receiver will get confused.

Netiquette suggests you avoid writing other people's e-mail addresses in your messages. This may cause someone else to receive **spam** and other unwanted e-mail.

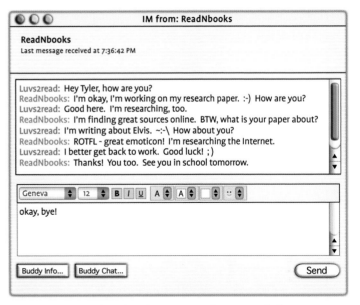

IM from: ReadNbooks

ReadNbooks
Last message received at 7:36:42 PM

Luvs2read: Hey Tyler, how are you?
ReadNbooks: I'm okay, I'm working on my research paper. :-) How are you?
Luvs2read: Good here. I'm researching, too.
ReadNbooks: I'm finding great sources online. BTW, what is your paper about?
Luvs2read: I'm writing about Elvis. ~:-\ How about you?
ReadNbooks: ROTFL - great emoticon! I'm researching the Internet.
Luvs2read: I better get back to work. Good luck! ;)
ReadNbooks: Thanks! You too. See you in school tomorrow.

Geneva   12   **B** *I* U A A

okay, bye!

Buddy Info...   Buddy Chat...   Send

Instant messaging is also a popular use of the Internet. This allows conversation to occur as fast as you type.

Another netiquette rule is not to type in all capital letters. IT LOOKS LIKE YOU'RE SHOUTING. This can be difficult to read and should be avoided. Also, try not to flame. This is writing something harsh or rude that may hurt someone's feelings.

Finally, don't copy other people's work. This is plagiarism, or stealing. Being a good netizen is just like being a good citizen. It is best to follow the same rules on the Internet that you would in your classroom.

Citing Sites

The Internet contains a lot of information. Web sites, newsgroups, and e-mail can be great for backing up a research paper. But, remember to avoid plagiarism.

Plagiarism is claiming someone else's words or ideas are

Plagiarism is a form of stealing. Remember to take detailed notes of where you get your information.

your own. You can use information from an e-mail or a Web page in a school report. However, you must then list it on a works cited page at the end of your paper. This is called citing a source.

Many schools require you to use the *MLA Handbook for Writers of Research Papers* when citing sources. It tells you what information to cite and how to organize it. This book can often be found at your local library.

The Internet can be a great tool when searching for information. Be sure to use it wisely and safely. If you have questions about searching the Internet, ask your teacher or librarian for help.

The Internet provides sources that may be difficult to find elsewhere. But, be sure to check Web site information against other sources for accuracy.

29

Glossary

access - the ability or permission to enter or use a place or thing.

accurate - free of errors.

bias - a leaning toward one side or point of view.

database - a large collection of information.

directory - an alphabetical list of names or addresses.

evaluate - to determine the meaning or importance of something.

graphic - of or relating to visual arts such as painting and photography.

hierarchical - organized according to rank or standing.

hyperlink - an electronic connection from one place in a hypertext document to another.

hypertext - a computer software feature that allows a user to select a word or item and link to additional information about it.

keywords - special phrases or words that narrow an Internet search.

network - a way to let computers share information.

nuclear - of or relating to the energy created when atoms are divided or combined.

online - connected to the Internet.

software - the written computer programs used by a computer.

spam - e-mail that is sent to a large number of addresses. Spam is usually sent by a business to a person who did not request it.

supercomputer - a large, very fast computer that can handle many tasks at once.

technology - using scientific knowledge for practical purposes, especially in industry.

hierarchical - heye-uh-RAHR-kih-kuhl
netiquette - NEH-tih-kuht
netizens - NEH-tuh-zuhnz
plagiarism - PLAY-juh-rih-zuhm

To learn more about the Internet, visit ABDO Publishing Company on the World Wide Web at **www.abdopub.com**. Web sites about the Internet are featured on our Book Links page. These links are routinely monitored and updated to provide the most current information available.

Index